Overcoming Distractions:

A Guide On How To Manage Your Time Wisely And Focus On Your Goal

By

Larry M. Barton

TABLE OF CONTENT

Introduction

Efficiency wouldn't be so difficult to accomplish, with the exception of the straightforward truth that we as a whole have a foe that continually attempts to bait us from doing and finishing our significant work. This foe? As a matter of fact, distraction. People are designed for distraction. Our mind's attentional framework is modified to answer whatever is pleasurable, undermining, or novel. We even have an oddity predisposition, wherein our cerebrum is overflowed with a delight compound, dopamine, whenever we center around a genuinely new thing.

As far as our developmental history, this appears to be legit. Rather than zeroing in solely on, say, lighting a fire, our old progenitors were occupied by external dangers — an approaching antagonist for instance — so they have to obliterate their prior goal

Chapter 1

Distraction; The Enemy Of An Achiever

We live in lousy times, more diverted than at any other time in recent memory. If you've attempted to have a discussion of late with somebody without them taking a look at their telephone, or replying before you complete your sentence then you understand what I mean. Yet, can we just look at things objectively, any one of us could be to blame for it?

Distraction is the incredible foe of progress.

At the point when we carry on with a diverted life, we carry on with a daily existence beyond the truth. Our brains meander and draw away from that which is. The present mindset takes a secondary lounge to a ceaseless coaxing somewhere else, to no place. Without reason and control. Our lives become a fence of minor, undefined, non-significant happenings. We exchange the truth of life for its insignificance. Nothing is hallowed, except the perpetual checking of online entertainment, texts, messages, and whatever else collects our restricted abilities to focus. Distraction is the foe of all that we want throughout everyday life. It is anything that stops us from seeking after our fantasies and completing what we long for. With each check of a text, with each wandering idea, with each shortfall of presence, except if it's serving our objective (and trust me, predominantly they're not), they're an obstruction and boundary to accomplishing what makes a difference to us. At the point when we're diverted, we lose center, and without concentration, nothing advantageous is feasible.

How then do we liberate ourselves from this plague of distraction? How would we beat it to understand the maximum capacity that exists in us? If focus is the way to progress, it makes sense that we should embrace an aptness for it. We should gain the self-restraint to say "no". No to sitting in front of the TV, no to taking a look at online entertainment, no to hopping upon every text, no to the time killers, and no to the people who would prefer to have us come up short than succeed. We should focus on those things that matter and be able to recognize them from the things that don't. If we're not in that frame of mind to do this, then all the work and sweat on the planet will be for no good reason.

The excellence of distraction is that it's inside our means to dispose of. We don't need to acknowledge it and we don't need to play it down. Sadly, an excessive number of us let it rule our lives, rather than us administering it. In any case, it doesn't need to be like that. In a free society where decisions are critical, we can decide to get rid of distractions. With a touch of self-discipline and assurance, an interruption-free life is our own to acquire.

Distractions stand at the entrance of your predetermination. They're in many cases little, however, the effect they have on your development is colossal. The little and ignored elements of distraction hold us back from going to a higher level. Distractions can appear in a wide range of structures. Furthermore, what we wanted in one season, maybe a distraction
for us in the following season. We can't necessarily in all cases control each Distraction that surfaces in our lives but you should have some control over your reaction and how you deal with those interruptions.

I can't predict the specific distractions
in your everyday indulgent, yet I can
give examples of probably the most
widely recognized;
Web-based Entertainment,
telephones, Hecticness, and
Performing multiple tasks which can
lead to a lack of focus
Our capacity to concentrate has
diminished because of the consistent
choices we have and the hustle of life.
The common mistake individuals
make while attempting to increase
their efficiency is not having an
understanding of what their
distractions are.

It proposes doing a time review by keeping a log of how you manage your time in your own and work life. After you do this, return and audit it to see where your time is going. Frequently, we will come to acknowledge we have much additional time to burn than we are aware of, yet the assignments are taking us longer than needed because of distractions.

One more distraction that frequently slips through the cracks is the distraction in our spirits. At the point when our lives are continually rushed, we're torn in such a large number of

bearings, consequently, we can't keep up. When you start to
recognize what distractions are a major part of your life, you can conquer them by making propensities to get you on a way of proficiency and reliable discernment.
Put yourself in a position for success by reclaiming your time. We just have a specific measure of hours in the day. We should not allow them to be taken away by the adversary called distraction.
I'm constantly stunned when I hear a person complains about the miserable state of his life. Then I observed more on the grumbler's ordinary

developments and energy center. I regularly witness activities like scrolling the Web as opposed to completing an assignment, messaging companions as opposed to settling on deals - - or occupying downtime with unscripted tv as opposed to putting resources into personal development. These are only a couple of distractions that waste our time and can enormously hurt an individual's chance of accomplishing his life goals.

Distractions aren't only the adversary for people, but also groups and associations. Every day, we are confronted with an endless number of distractions with the tendency to adversely affect our efficiency.

How to mitigate Distraction

Numerous things in life can, possibly, burn through a great deal of time. By limiting distractions and eliminating time-squanderers from our day, we can achieve more and possibly become more effective.

1. Remain mission-centered: As people, we long for significance and satisfaction, and one of the speediest ways of accomplishing that and at the same time limit interruptions is to remain mission centered in all we do.

It's not difficult to get up every morning and make a cursory effort, however, when you stay mission-centered, Distractions can not find expression. To help yourself in such a manner, post your statement of purpose where you can see it during the day. I have my assertion on my PC, on my telephone, and on a notecard, which I have with me wherever I go. This powers me to continually remain mission-centered and overlook the "clamor" that surfaces over the day. At the point when we don't remain mission-centered,

Distractions interfere more regularly. Individuals fail to remember for what reason they're here or where they're going because they've become derailed

2. Comprehend and examine your flimsy spots: A valuable activity for me was the time I gave an entire end of the week to break down the greatest distractions hindering my steps to attaining my goals. I was feeling disappointed and useless so I invested energy in going through my everyday daily practice and

timetable and following
precisely the way my time was
being spent. I at long last had the
option to be straightforward with
myself and pinpointed three key
distractions that had been
keeping me from getting my
most significant undertakings
and tasks done. I didn't know
about them before I rolled out
certain improvements. You don't
need to spend the whole end of
the week investigating your
greatest distractions, yet spend
no less than 20 minutes and see
what you can do less over the
day that will create more time to

spend on things that make the biggest difference. The vast majority don't do this. Be that as it may, assuming you do, you'll understand what your obstructions have been.

3. Discipline yourself by creating a schedule that you plan to be serious with: The simplest method for battling distractions is to plan the main tasks and work that need your attention every day. Something that has functioned admirably for me is time-hindering, which involves returning to my foundations as a

competitor when I had a ludicrously focused plan and the entire day shut out. At the point when you dedicate a period in which you commit yourself to an important task, distractions and "commotion" are extraordinarily limited. The prior night, plan your following day, shutting out your most significant errands and needs. This will incite you to get up in the early hours of the day Because you have an outline, and something critical that you want to take care of. Consistently, countless people are misled by the upheaval and breaks in their lives. All things considered, be conscious. Discard the distraction that doesn't fill a more prominent need.

4. Awareness Meditation: There are two methods for diminishing distraction: by removing the root of the distraction or internally by expanding your capacity to concentrate. To boost your capacity to diminish distractions you have to consolidate both internal and outward procedures.

Awareness meditation, like different types of meditation, helps quiet the brain and this further improves focus. Furthermore, what awareness meditation is excellent at is giving us lucidity of the brain.

5. Alter your social use to match objectives: The thought here is to adjust the virtual entertainment you continuously consume to match what you're attempting to achieve. This could mean reducing the amount of social media content you consume every day if it

represents a distraction. You should delete an app or block a website if push comes to shove. On the other hand, you can alter your social use by unfollowing unprofitable platforms and attaching yourself to positive social influences who will offer messages that will persuade and rouse you to activity.

6. Rise early: The calm of the early morning is by a wide margin the most useful time for me. Also, it's not simply me, rising early has ended up being ridiculously famous with a myriad of

published books expressing this phenomenon. Most resources you'll see out there will instruct you to rise at a very unusual time, however, all you have to do is try to rise as early as you can. Rising thirty minutes to 60 minutes earlier than usual will allow you to either finish some work or plan for the day ahead with a couple of wake-up routines, making you significantly more viable in all that you do through the remainder of your day.

7. Utilize miniature prizes: Every night, I take myself out to eat my favorite delicacy and have a walk down the park with my dog. Why is this significant? It serves as a form of motivation. Each day I am motivated to do a great job so that I can enjoy his favorite meal. Using this kind of reward system is very effective and easy to use in your own life. Consider your very own miniature compensation. It doesn't need to be related to food like mine, it very well may be any sort of little enjoyment that gives you joy. Then utilize this

as a prize for a hard day's worth
of effort and perceive how it
further develops your
concentration daily.

Utilize these seven methods to lessen
distraction, develop concentration,
and get more work done. Find which
one works for you, and find your
ideal arrangement of methodologies
and strategies that permits you to go
about your responsibilities every day.

Chapter 2

Causes Of Distractions

There is this common perception that there isn't enough time. Yet, the majority of us burn through an additional amount of time every week than we want to concede. The ideal timewaster is charming, permits an opportunity to fly by, and is profoundly diverting.

Nowadays, we have a myriad of distractions that fit the bill of an ideal distraction. Timewasters are generally propensities that give next to zero significant compensation for the time contributed.

Keep away from these timewasters and you'll add more hours to your day to do what matters the most;

1. Overthinking: There's no proof that your considerations influence the outer world. You can stress all you want over the climate, your obligation, or your relationship. Worrying causes physical and emotional pressure. It likewise makes you less useful

and less fit for managing the issue.

2. Compulsiveness: Ask yourself how expertly something should be done and endeavor to accomplish that degree of value. Flawlessness is an unimaginable objective and calls for undeniably more investment than it's worth.

3. Electronic gadgets: This includes your phone, your TV, and any other gadgets that incite addiction. Some people spend the whole day on the sofa

watching people while others can't do away with their phones. That being said, they are a source of distraction even for serious-minded people

4. Social media: In principle, web-based entertainment is something extraordinary. But, practically speaking, it requires a ton of investment and produces pressure.

5. Staying aware of your life: Some things must be done that don't improve our day-to-day routines yet simply keep up with

our lives. This incorporates undertakings like shopping, cooking, cleaning, clothing, cooking, and taking care of the lawn. If conceivable, pay others to play out these assignments for you.

6. Uncertainty: If you lack direction, you're probably going to sit idle. Figure out how to rapidly decide. Settle on the most ideal choice you can and start working on it immediately

7. Gatherings or meetings: Numerous gatherings are an

exercise in futility, and they can suck the satisfaction from your spirit. An insufficient gathering is more regrettable than not having a gathering by any stretch of the imagination. Plan fittingly for useful gatherings and attempt to keep away from the rest.

8. No arrangement for the afternoon: Having an arrangement for the next day before you sleep is a good method to save time. Create a plan around evening time and afterward go through the day working on your plan.

9. Weariness: It's difficult to go about your best responsibilities while tired. You work more slowly, commit more errors, and have a diminished capacity to concentrate and use sound judgment. Get your rest

Clinical reasons for Distractions

Distraction isn't shallow. It has a more profound significance, which is the reason it will be better for your psychological prosperity if you address it earliest.

Distraction is a psychological state! Do you generally lose your chain of thought? Do your associates and individual mates generally find you wandering off in fantasy land? You need to genuinely investigate the matter. This probably won't cost you only your efficiency but your psychological prosperity as well. Being consistently distracted isn't healthy.

Distraction can be brought about by many reasons; that you haven't eaten your dinner appropriately, assuming something is winding in your mind, assuming you are emotionally scarred.

Weariness is a widespread encounter;
we all have felt it in our way. There
will never be a solitary day that
possibly we or another person hasn't
said 'I'm exhausted,"
He adds, "Yet weariness is a horde of
perplexing sentiments and feelings,
it's considerably more than sitting
around aimlessly or lethargy and it's
the commonest reason for getting
diverted."

**Here are a few noticeable
explanations behind distractions
that you may overlook**

1. Assuming you are managing psychological wellness issues like nervousness, misery, dyslexia, consideration shortfall/hyperactivity jumble (ADHD), and so forth, it appears to be that distraction turns into its side effect.

2. At the point when you are genuinely delaying an excessive lot, you for the most part feel dist. Fundamentally, when you are sincerely depleted, you continue to stack up stuff and leave it for the latest possible second. That happens because stalling causes you to feel tired

and doesn't allow you to zero in appropriately on anything.

3. when we don't feel rested enough or when the tasks we are performing have become repetitive, it frames a dreary pattern of conduct.

4. At the point when we are caught in a consistent, ceaseless circle of deadlines with no genuine break, it prompts irritation and disappointment.

5. when we can't concentrate because of decreased capacity to focus in certain conditions like attention deficit disorder (ADD)

6. when we need more inspiration or the undertaking isn't compensating enough.

7. One more main explanation for distraction is performing multiple tasks. If you are doing an excessive number of things in one go, there are high possibilities that you can not zero in on a certain something, particularly, intellectually. You feel overpowered constantly and unfit to perform to your full limit.

A few fast hacks to manage it

1. Taking care of oneself (everyday practice): Carve out opportunities to deal with your physical and emotional well-being like daily exercise, eating on time, and sufficient rest.
2. Switch your everyday practice: Break your pattern of weariness and track down imaginative approaches to playing out your day-to-day work
3. Counsel a psychologist to resolve any issues concerning your emotional and psychological well-being: Therapy for the brain resembles

a spa for the body and
contemplation for the psyche.

The point that you want to note here
is that you should be extremely
certain about your psychological
prosperity. You can't stand to
relinquish a solitary sign, regardless
of whether it is as innocuous as a
distraction.

CHAPTER 3

How To Maintain Focus And Concentrate

Concentration and fixation can be hard to dominate. Indeed, many people need to figure out how to further develop concentration and lift focus. However, We live in a loud world and steady interruptions make concentration a difficulty

What then is Focus?

Focus can happen when we have expressed yes to one choice and no to any remaining choices. As such, discipline is necessary for focus to take place. Focus doesn't need a permanent no, however, it requires a present no. You generally have the choice to accomplish something different later, however, right now focus expects that you just do a certain thing. Focus is the way to efficiency since expressing no to every other choice opens your capacity to achieve the one thing that is left.

Presently for the significant inquiry: How can we zero in on the things that matter and disregard the things that don't?

Why is it difficult to remain focused?

A lot of people don't experience difficulty with concentration. They experience difficulty with choosing. What I mean is that most people have a mind that is fit for focusing assuming we move the distractions . Have you at any point had an assignment that you needed to finish? What was the deal? You made it happen because the cutoff time pursued the choice for you. Perhaps you procrastinated ahead of time, yet when things became dire and you had to settle on a choice, you made a move.

Rather than accomplishing the troublesome work of picking one thing to focus on, we frequently persuade ourselves that performing various tasks is a superior choice. This is futile. However, we can do two things simultaneously. It is conceivable, for instance, to stare at the television while preparing a meal or to answer an email while chatting on the telephone. What is inconceivable, is focusing on two tasks without a moment's delay.

You're either paying attention to the television and the meal you're preparing is a commotion, or you're watching out for the cooking pot and the television is a disturbance. Performing multiple tasks powers your cerebrum to switch your concentration here and there, rapidly starting with one assignment and then onto the next. This wouldn't be anything serious if the human cerebrum would change flawlessly starting with one work and then onto the next, yet it can't.

Have you at any point been busy composing an email when somebody cuts your attention? At the point when the discussion is finished and you return to the message, it takes you a couple of moments to recall what you were composing, and refocus. Performing various tasks compels you to follow through at a psychological cost each time you hinder one errand and leap to another. In psychology, this cost is known as the switching cost.

Switching cost is the interruption in execution that we experience when we change our concentration from one thing to another. According to a study, it requires 64 seconds to continue with the task you were doing before you checked your email.

Concentrate on the process, Not the Occasion

What can do to endure your concentration is to focus on the processes, not on occasions. Time and again, we see a positive outcome as an occasion that can be accomplished and finished.

Here are a few instances:

Many individuals consider well-being to be an occasion: "On the off chance that I simply shed 28 pounds, then, at that point, I'll be in shape."

Many individuals consider business to be an occasion: "if our business is highlighted in the wall street journal, then, we're good to go"

Many individuals consider craftsmanship to be an occasion: "On the off chance that I could simply get my work highlighted in a greater display, then, at that point, I'd have the validity I want."

Those are only a couple of the numerous ways that we order accomplishment as a solitary occasion. In any case, assuming you observe individuals who keep fixed on their objectives, you begin to understand that not the occasions or the outcomes make them unique. It's the obligation to the cycle. They

become enamored with the everyday
practice, not the singular occasion.

What's interesting is that this
attention to the cycle will permit you
to partake in the outcomes in any
case.
To be an extraordinary essayist, then
having a smash hit book is
magnificent. However, the best way
to arrive at that outcome is to become
hopelessly enamored with the most
common way of composing.
If you believe that the world should
be aware of your business, then it is
only right it's featured in Forbes
magazine. In any case, the best way

to arrive at that outcome is to be interested in the most common way of promotion.

If you want the best body shape, then shedding 20 pounds may be fundamental. But, the best way to arrive at that outcome is to love the most common way of practicing good eating habits and exercising frequently.

To turn out to be essentially better at anything, you need to develop an interest in the simplest way of getting it done. You need to become enamored with building the personality of somebody who accomplishes the work, instead of

simply dreaming about your desired
outcomes

Zeroing in on results and objectives is
our normal propensity, however,
focusing on processes will eventually
produce our desired outcome

Fixation Psyche Hacks

Indeed, even after you've figured out
how to adore the processes and ability
to remain fixed on your objectives,
the everyday execution of those
objectives can in any case be
muddled. We should discuss other
ways of further developing fixation

and ensure you're genuinely focusing on each work.

Instructions to Further develop Fixation

The following are other ways to develop your focus and get started with what makes a difference.

1. Pick a Priority task: One of the significant upgrades I've made lately is to prioritize the single most important work for the day. Even though I intend to finish different tasks during the day, my needful task is the one non-debatable thing that must be

done. I consider this my "priority task" since it is the backbone of my working hours. The advantage of picking one priority task is that it directs your way of behaving by constraining you to arrange your life around that obligation

2. Deal with your energy: When an errand requires your complete focus, fix it to a time when you have the energy to focus. For instance, I have seen that my innovative energy is most elevated toward the beginning of the day. That is the point at

which I put forth a valiant effort to work. That is the point at which I settle on the best conclusions about my business: Anyway, what do I do? I plan essential tasks for the first part of the day. Any remaining business assignments are dealt with in the early evening. Practically, every efficiency methodology fixates on dealing with your time better, however, time is futile if you don't have the energy you want to finish the job you are chipping away at.

3. Never browse email before the early afternoon: Social media can be one of the greatest interruptions of all. If I don't browse email towards the start of the day, then I'm ready to go through the early morning seeking after my plan as opposed to responding to every other person's plan. That is great since I'm not squandering mental energy pondering on every one of the messages in my inbox. I understand that holding on until midday isn't doable for some individuals, however, I want to offer a test. Shouldn't something

be said about 9AM? 8:30AM? The specific deadline doesn't make any difference. The point is to cut out time during your morning when you can focus on what means quite a bit to you without letting the remainder of the world direct your psychological state.

4. Drop your telephone in another room: I ordinarily don't see my telephone in the early mornings of the day. It is a lot simpler to accomplish your work when you have no instant messages, calls,

or cautions intruding on your concentration.

5. Work in full-screen mode: Whenever I utilize an application on my PC, I utilize full-screen mode. Assuming that I'm perusing an article on the web, my program takes up the entire screen. Assuming that I'm typing on MS word, I'm working in full-screen mode. I have set up my work area so the menu bar vanishes naturally. At the point when I'm working, I can't see the time, the symbols of different applications, or some

other interruptions on the screen. It's interesting how much difference this makes for my concentration and fixation. If you can see a symbol on your screen, then you will be reminded to tap on it at times. In any case, if you eliminate the viewable prompt, the desire to be diverted dies down in almost no time.

6. Eliminate all works that could interrupt you from focusing in the morning: I love doing the main thing first every day because the urgencies of the day

have not sneaked in yet. I have gone a little far in such that I have even pushed my most memorable feast off until about early afternoon every day. I have been discontinuous fasting for two years at this point, and that implies that I normally eat the greater part of my feast somewhere in the range of 12 PM and 7 PM. The outcome is that I get an extra opportunity in the first part of the day to accomplish important work as opposed to preparing breakfast.

Notwithstanding what guide you use, simply recall that whenever you find the world diverting you, you should simply focus on a certain something. First and foremost, you don't for a moment even need to succeed. You simply have to begin.

Chapter 4

Managing Your Time With Great Mastery

It's the main asset we have — and one that can't be acquired, or paused. Whether we're bankrupt or on the Forbes rundown of tycoons, everyone gets precisely the same measure of it every day.
Are you making the most of the time allocated to you?

Managing your time expertly is often based on propensities and schedules. evaluating your pattern of behavior and handling your time usage proactively will work on virtually every part of your life.

We can't do everything, except with the right demeanor but we can do significantly more than we're doing at present. We can live more joyful, and more useful lives. Also, we can let loose valuable minutes to loosen up and invest time with our friends and family.

What does it mean to use time productively?

The vast majority comprehend the significance of dealing with their time, however, they're mulling over everything in the incorrect manner. Completion of a task is a pivotal piece of time productivity — yet it's only one of many. In the present time of limitless decisions and interruptions, knowing what not to do is comparably significant. We likewise must be careful that the undertakings we focus on are lined up with our greatest objectives. Why bother with figuring out how to run quicker assuming you're dashing off base?

A strong time usage methodology is about arranging the cards to pursue the ideal decisions as frequently as possible. The most important phase in creating one is the awareness of how you're investing your energy at present. A precise pattern will give you the lucidity you need to move along.

Understanding Where Your Times Goes.

How long did you spend on messages today?

For the majority of us, this kind of inquiry is hard to respond to. We get so submerged in anything we're doing right now that we lose viewpoint.

This prompts an incorrect impression of our general efficiency. Therefore, our time usage strategies may likely not improve. We could attempt to fix issues that don't exist, or on the other hand, disregard genuine ones.

To be adept at using time productively, you must comprehend where your time goes now.

There are a lot of simple methods for doing this. Rather than attempting to stay aware of everything all alone, you could utilize a time-tracking application or software such as RescueTime or Toggl track. After you've followed your time for half a month, you'll be compelled to address old suspicions. Get ready to be stunned at how long you're spending on apparently harmless activities like emails or web-based entertainment. You'll see specific activities, times, and conditions helpful for top efficiency (as well as the other way around).

Heads up ahead of time

Following your time may be awkward. Assuming you're deterred by that multitude of squandered minutes, cheer up because they're all only chances to develop. Figuring out how long you spend doing things will assist you with improving as an assessor while arranging your daily routine — significant time-usage expertise.

Plan your time by preparing an objective survey- Focusing on Your Time

Not all works are made equivalent. How you esteem them relies upon your definitive objectives. If it's your main goal this year to complete your most memorable long-distance race, for example, a long run may be one of the foundations of your day. Be that as it may, somebody attempting to begin a side business despite having a day job could need to make do with a speedy yoga exercise all things being equal.

Powerful time usage begins with a reasonable vision of your objectives and values. Hustling through twelve minor errands may be less significant than a solitary troublesome one that is more lined up with your vision.

The differentiation between dire and significant undertakings can be unobtrusive, yet significant. It's so natural to go through a whole day answering messages, having a gathering, and obliging others' plans at the expense of your objectives. extinguishing a fire is vital, however, it shouldn't come at the cost of the genuinely significant stuff.

The simplest ways to make smart choices daily? attempt proven time usage procedures and strategies.

Time Usage Procedures and Strategies

Many of us could tolerate managing our time better. Yet, our difficulties are extraordinary. A few of us battle choice weakness and tiredness. Others are in a steady fight with laziness and procrastination. The best time usage procedure for you may not

work for others; work style and
character makes the difference
That is the reason I have separated the
most widely recognized time usage
issues into four classifications and
suggested various systems for each.

1. Choice Weakness: Every day
   expects us to decide on a huge
   number of choices. Some are
   little, similar to what to wear to
   work, or have for lunch. Others
   are bigger, either to stand up to a
   collaborator or ask your manager
   for a raise. Every one of them
   drainingly affects our restricted
   resolution.

The outcome? Choice exhaustion. It gets increasingly hard to use sound judgment as the day goes on. Therefore, it may be very difficult to conclude what to do at the very moment

Follow these guidelines to over choice weakness

- Try not to Break the Chain: It takes a strong mind to decide, provided that those choices are cognizant. The more brilliant decisions you can imbibe as propensities, the simpler it is to redo them while keeping away from choice exhaustion. You don't have to contemplate them. On the off chance that you're attempting to fabricate each new propensity, this technique is straightforward and viable. Seeing every one of the red imprints on your schedule is inspiring. When the new way of behaving becomes propensity, you can continue to fabricate another with a lot of self-discipline in excess.

- To avoid Records: You've presumably used a to-do list before. In any case, consider the possibility that you flipped the cycle on its head and made an alternate rundown of patterns of behavior to stay away from. That is the overall thought behind avoiding records. To begin with, distinguish your greatest efficiency traps. These will ordinarily be things like web-based entertainment, browsing messages, and superfluous gatherings. Presently it turns into your main goal to stay away from anything on this rundown list. This time usage method is extraordinary because it eliminates the pressure of flawlessness. Rather than attempting to do an entire pack of new things, you're just doing less to plug those efficiency spills.

2. Setting Cutoff times: The vast majority of us disdain cutoff times since we partner them with stress and sensations of frailty. We're compelled to squeeze our work into our managers' or clients' timetables rather than our own. Therefore, we'd try not to bring much more cutoff times into our lives. Be that as it may, situations become different when the cutoff times are purposeful. Rather than a source of stress,

setting our cutoff times for choices can come with a sense of liberation. We don't need to ponder on the thing any longer. We act, and afterward, we can continue with our lives. Setting cutoff times and keeping to them helps us to make decisions rapidly in the foreseeable future. We get better at it and gain certainty after some time. These are extremely valuable abilities for dealing with the unusualness of the everyday.

3. Time-Hindering: If you have something to do but you're

uncertain about when to do it, time-hindering can help. This method is straightforward: split your days into halves and allocate specific tasks to each. You can utilize a schedule application or make your time blocks by hand by sharing bits of lined journal paper. Assuming during the day, something surprising comes up, you can constantly modify the leftover time blocks and continue to move. Time-hindering is incredible because it compels you to assess what amount of time each errand will require.

You'll get better at it over the long run, and it becomes simpler to make arrangements over time. You don't have to stress yourself about what to do next, the choice has already been made; you should simply follow your task blocks.

4. Being Overwhelmed: Pressure is the norm in the present society. There's such a great amount of work to do — and not sufficient opportunity to get them done. Also, you may have difficulty investing your time because of interruptions, and interferences.

In the event that you're battling with a pressed timetable or can't sort out what to do straightaway, check these time usage techniques out.

1. Brief Life: Brief Life is similarly straightforward as it gets. A method that involves 7 minutes every morning and 7 minutes at night, a sum of one percent of your time. You'll utilize your morning minutes to prepare for the day. In the night, you'll survey how you did and plan for the following day. Made by monetary guide Allyson Lewis,

this framework is perfect for
individuals who don't normally
design their time or who are still
attempting to sort out their
objectives. It's straightforward,
so it shouldn't be a big deal

2. Eisenhower Network: The
Eisenhower Network, advocated
by the well-known Second Great
War general and U.S. president,
is a rich instrument to focus on
your tasks. list the tasks that you
need to attend to. Note which
ones are pressing and significant,

or insignificant. Then, group your assignments into four classes:

Dire and significant tasks — do these tasks right away

Significant, however not pressing — plan these tasks for a later date

Pressing but not significant — these assignments need to be done but don't have to be by you. Verify whether you can robotize, delegate, or re-appropriate them so you can zero in on what's significant.

Not pressing and insignificant —
overlook or keep away from your task
list t

The objective is to invest more
energy in the initial two
classifications and less attention in
the second two classifications. At the
point when you're confronted with a
considerable rundown of errands, the
Eisenhower Grid is an extraordinary
method for isolating the good product
from the debris.

3. Most Significant Assignments:
   The majority of us are very
   bright at the beginning of our

day. Our determination is at its
pinnacle, and every one of the
day's distractions hasn't gotten
an opportunity to strike. You can
utilize this period to distinguish
and finish your most significant
task. Utilize the nights to list
your main three to five important
tasks for the following day.
Begin the following morning
with your most important task.
You can constantly push back
tasks you weren't able to
complete to the following day.

4. Tarrying: Knowing what needs
   to be done is unfortunately not

enough. If we can't move past that obstruction against beginning an errand, we may never complete it. you don't have to become mixed up in an extra one-hour perusing meeting on Twitter. Check these tips out to beat lingering;

5. Self-adjust: Self-adjust is an incredible time usage procedure if you're battling with low inspiration. Rather than compelling yourself to accomplish something you fear, make a rundown of activities and begin with anything you're

generally intrigued by. The thought here is to simply begin with a task. You'll get energy as you continue. At the point when you follow through with your ongoing task or end up getting exhausted, switch over to one more thing on the rundown that has you interested. You can return to it later on. Don't continue exchanging and adding tasks endlessly. Ensure you finish anything that you start on your underlying rundown before you add more.

6. Piecing: Nobody wants to take a look at their plan for the day and see "compose a sales report of the past 6 months." That sounds too overpowering to even consider beginning. So you end up stalling and worrying. This is where piecing comes in. It's a basic system to separate complex tasks into sensible pieces. In the first place, drill down all the actionable steps that will bring about the completed item. You'll likely begin to feel better after that. Start with the beginning steps and complete them immediately. You could in

any case have a ton of work to do, yet you've made a guide for yourself now. Essentially you've begun!

7. To-do list: Plans for the day are exemplary time usage strategies. Certain individuals love them, while others can't stand them. The greatest advantage of to-do lists is moving that large number of tumultuous contemplations in your mind into something methodical on paper. You'll in any case need to focus on when to do them, but understanding what you have before you is a

significant improvement. You can utilize antiquated pen and paper or go virtual. A lot of instruments and applications are accessible on the web.

Effectiveness

Understanding what to do and when to do it is perfect. But it isn't worth a lot without the capacity to execute

Check these tips out if you're unable to be productive.

1. Computerize Repeating tasks: It's already hard to overcome our

tasks every day without pestering reminders to pay the lease or send a receipt. You can utilize innovation to deal with these common errands, opening up valuable energy to zero in on whatever needs full focus.

Here are only a couple of tasks you could robotize:

- Backing up your information
- Keeping a part of your paycheck in an investment account
- Covering bills
- Answering messages with canned formats
- Schedule arrangements

- Social media posts
- Arranging your emails
- Clumping

Clumping is the most common way of collecting related tasks and taking them out at the same time. Rather than cooking consistently, for example, you could do some mass feast preparation on Sunday night and not stress over it the remainder of the week. You could commit specific time allotments to clear your email inbox. Clumping makes you more productive because you limit the mental expenses of exchanging to and fro between tasks.

2. Pomodoro Procedure: The Pomodoro Procedure, named after the tomato-formed clock ("pomodoro" is tomato in Italian) its maker utilized while creating it. It separates your work into committed pieces and breaks. This assists you with remaining focused without getting worn out. The standard Pomodoro work block is 25 minutes of continuous work, trailed by a 5-minute break. Whenever you've rehearsed three or four of these blocks, you can enjoy some time off (10 to

30 minutes) before accomplishing any more work. You can change the proportions of work to break time also. Longer work periods (like 50 minutes on to 10 minutes off) will give you additional opportunities to submerge yourself in confounded tasks. Go ahead and analyze and figure out what turns out best for you.

3. Plan Breaks: This sounds strange. How could you need to plan non-work time assuming you're attempting to be more useful? Planning breaks between

tasks keeps up with fixation and productivity. Indeed, even the most focused individuals can't remain on track for a whole business day. Without consistently booked breaks, you risk remaining submerged in something until you become occupied and wasteful. Breaks give you something to anticipate — and an opportunity to re-energize. What amount of time you need for your breaks depends on you. Try to sort out how much work you can deal with on the go before you take a rest. That takes some testing.

www.ingramcontent.com/pod-product-compliance
Lightning Source LLC
Chambersburg PA
CBHW050817250726

48653CB00006B/2278